T0113542

Why the
# Black
# Church
*Has*
# FAILED

*Why the* **Black Church** *Has* **FAILED**

Nathaniel Wilson

WESTBOW
PRESS®
A DIVISION OF THOMAS NELSON
& ZONDERVAN

WestBow Press books may be ordered through booksellers or by contacting:

WestBow Press
A Division of Thomas Nelson & Zondervan
1663 Liberty Drive
Bloomington, IN 47403
www.westbowpress.com
1 (866) 928-1240

ISBN: 978-1-9736-0783-0 (sc)
ISBN: 978-1-9736-0784-7 (e)

Library of Congress Control Number: 2017917635

Print information available on the last page.

WestBow Press rev. date: 12/1/2017

# INTRODUCTION

At least once a week, usually on Sunday, people all across the nation and around the world gather together in the name of Christianity in order to participate in an organized worship service. Although they all claim to be legitimate churches, why are they so vastly different? Why is there such an enormous difference in worship/meeting styles? Is there one church or many? Is there one head of the church or many? The church seems to have raised more questions than it has provided answers. If you have had difficulty in finding a church that you like, then you're just not looking hard enough because there is a church on almost every corner with almost as many different beliefs and styles.

Church styles range from one end of the spectrum where you have the extremely laid back, where there is a motionless, almost completely silent gathering, to the other end of the spectrum that is characterized by a completely off the chain, over the top, all the way to the wall, knock-down drag-out emotional experience. Since this is the case, then surely you can find a church among them that you're comfortable with, if you're really looking for one. It seems to me that these differences in worship styles indicate that they originate from the worshippers rather than from the one being worshipped.

Wouldn't the one being worshipped have the right to determine what it is that truly constitutes true worship of himself? Yes, he does, and yes, he has. We only need to look at the scriptures, where God has given us very clear information as to what coming together to worship him should look like. However, the variety of styles indicates that we have rejected that information, and we've created a style of worship that suits us. And since different peoples have different backgrounds and different cultures, we seem to have made a priority of designing worship styles that allow us to be comfortable in our individual traditions, at the expense of preventing impartial truth from coming forth.

In the case of the black church (which I have had many years to experience firsthand), it has been the display of extreme uncontrollable emotion that has defined our worship services. Our style of gathering in the black church is very lively and noisy. There is considerable movement, swaying and rocking; there is also much standing, shouting, and vocal expression. It seems that the main objective in our churches is not to have the people be spiritually edified by the Word of God through preaching and teaching but rather to just enjoy a very highly entertaining, somewhat theater-like performance by the pastor and choir. The goal is to maintain for the next thirty to ninety minutes the highest emotional experience possible through the music, the preaching, the singing, and the testifying. But the question is, is this kind of activity, behavior, and mind-set consistent with God's expressed expectation of those of us who claim to assemble in his name? All scripture references are taken from the KJV Bible.

# 1

# LET'S TAKE ANOTHER LOOK

Obviously, it is not my intention here to paint all black churches with such a broad brush. But we have many churches, and I'm afraid most have failed miserably in their attempts to be legitimate. These organizations are totally confused and have completely missed the mark as far as what the church truly is, what the church is really about, and what the church is actually supposed to be doing, according to the scripture.

As the son of a black pastor, I have been a part of the black church all my life. I have had literally my entire life to experience, observe, and be involved in practically every type of service there is. My experience in the black church consists of being totally consumed with and completely engulfed by every aspect of it. I've been a Sunday school teacher, Sunday school superintendent, deacon, Bible institute instructor, choir member, musician, choir director, and minister of music. About the only thing I haven't done is serve as a pastor, although I have worked very closely with pastors, including my father.

I have truly seen it all in the black church. The ins, the outs, the in-betweens, the ups, the downs, the all-arounds, the suspicious, the unexplained, and the unexpected. I've seen the whys, the why-nots, the what-fors, and the what-ifs. I've seen the whats, the nos, and the "You've gotta be kidding mes." You name it, and I've either experienced it or seen it—up close. So when it comes to the black church, yes, I guess you could say I have literally seen it all.

Growing up in the black church, I became fully acquainted with its philosophy and theology, what drives it, and what motivates it. But over time, I became more of a student of the scriptures, always desiring to increase my knowledge and, more importantly, my understanding of the Word of God, specifically those things relating to the church. I began to notice an enormous difference between the church I was seeing in the scriptures and the churches I had been a part of as I grew into adulthood. As a result, I was forced to make a choice between the two—at least in my heart and mind at that time.

If we use the scripture as our standard, then we will have to admit that the church today is confused—and the black church is absolutely confused. It is confused in that, although it claims to be the church, it is engaged in something that is totally foreign to and completely out of character with the church of scripture. Pastors and leaders of the black churches have completely rejected the very clear instructions that have been given to the church. Instead, the black church has taken the culture, experience, and tradition of its people, unique as it is, and has elevated those things above the truth of the Word of God. It has never become the true church of scripture.

The black church has basically substituted emotionalism and entertainment for true biblical worship and ministry. In many of our places of worship, neither Christ nor the Word of God is exalted or honored. From what I have witnessed over the years, I can say that the black church in general is a total and complete failure, according to the scripture. What goes on during its services is not at all biblical; it is far from it. But who cares about what the scripture says, right? So I have one question to the black church. Church? Just what in the world do you think you are doing? Whatever it is, it is certainly not legitimate Christian ministry.

For the most part, the black church service is nothing more than an emotional and entertaining gathering where everybody comes together just to have a good time. The church, whether it is black, white, or any other color—or any other way you wish to classify it—has no right to deviate from its scriptural mandate. Nor does it have the authority to create its own agenda. God has already laid it out for us. But sadly, that is exactly what the black church has done and continues to do.

Clearly, in the black church, the Word of God has simply been ignored or abused. Pastors and church leaders quote the scripture but have completely misused and misrepresented the scripture. Instead of allowing the scriptures to define and explain their experiences and traditions, leaders of the black church have used their experiences and traditions to define the scriptures. It's clear to see that according to the scripture, the black church—despite its legitimate appearance and widespread appeal—is involved in nothing more than absolute, spiritually meaningless activity. Sadly, our places of worship cannot be referred to as churches but religious entertainment centers because they do not bear even the slightest resemblance to the church of scripture.

Our churches do not have a clue, and I honestly don't believe they want one. They just simply want to remain what they are and what they have always been. The black church has certified, legitimized, and validated itself and, in so doing, has not sought the approval of the Word of God. Instead, it continues to seek the approval of the people as it always has. I encourage *you,* dear reader, to get into the Word of God. Read for yourself, study for yourself, and think for yourself.

# 2

# THE GREAT DECEPTION

For decades, our pastors and church leaders have either deliberately or unknowingly but enthusiastically promoted the idea that true spirituality is measured by the level of emotional expression during the church service. We have been taught that in order to be legitimate at church, both the preacher and the congregation must demonstrate a certain high degree of emotion, if we truly are Christians. And because of this kind of thinking, there has been—and continues to be—a push for the sensational, the entertaining, and the stirring of the emotions. These things may have helped our ancestors deal with the horrible things they had to endure, but even then it was not scriptural, nor is it now.

We have failed to truly study the scriptures for ourselves and consequentially have failed to see that this attitude and behavior is not what experiencing God is all about. Our tradition and culture has such a powerful grip on us that it prevents us from opening our eyes to the truth of the Word of God. We have deliberately chosen to remain in the dark about the true nature of the church of scripture. This mentality persists, even though the very clear truth of the Word of God is so abundantly available to us today. Our people have been completely misled and deceived for too long, and it is time that this false teaching that has gone under the pretense of biblical truth comes to an end. God, please help us.

This deception has gone on for so long that it now seems that we have fine-tuned our taste for this erroneous doctrine, and as a result, our desire for it has increased to the point that we now want nothing less than for it to continue. It is as if it has become part of our spiritual DNA. It's in our spiritual genes. So the pastors are pleased to continue to give it to us, and they do it for at least two reasons: First, they know that if they don't, then the people will go down the street to the other church because they know they can get it there. And second, the pastors themselves have been deceived and are convinced that what they are conveying is biblical truth. After all, they are passing on to their congregation the knowledge that has been passed down to them—the same knowledge that has been passed down for generations. For these same reasons, pastors will never genuinely consider consulting the scriptures when seeking guidance, direction, and instruction on how to carry out a legitimate ministry. They would never allow something like the Bible to do away with the church traditions that our ancestors have handed down to us. I must say that it is truly amazing to me to be able to experience something like this firsthand.

There are individuals who have left some of our churches

because they came to recognize all of this as the ministry of deception that it truly is, but most continue to attend. There are some who have a slight sense that something is wrong, but others are completely oblivious to the fact that they are receiving total error. I believe that some pastors and leaders, for fear that people will mature and grow and become less dependent on them, actually suppress, hide, and withhold the truth while promoting this false message. The black church as a whole has sadly bought in to this massive deception campaign and has failed to realize that it has been horribly deceived by its pastors and leaders.

Our people are fully capable of understanding the truth of God's Word, but we are not encouraged to study the Word for ourselves but only to believe what we are told. And since tradition, friendship, kinship, and culture have such a powerful hold on us, we just believe what we are told. We believe anything they tell us because we don't believe they would steer us in the wrong direction. I believe this is why the adversary is such a master at using all of these things in his grand scheme to deceive.

To our spiritual detriment, we refuse to read, think, and study for ourselves simply because a pastor or teacher convinces us that he or she is the only scriptural authority we need. We seem to be so easily deceived. The adversary is clever, but even as skillful as he is, I continue to be amazed at the believer's susceptibility to be tricked by him and at the ease with which he does it. In Ephesians 4:11–14, the apostle Paul informs members of the body of Christ of what we have been given in order to guard against deception.

As I talk with some individuals, they somehow sense that there may be something that is not quite right with what they are hearing, but they can't put their finger on what it is, so they continue to attend. They keep saying amen, they keep saying Hallelujah, and they keep shouting, because what they are hearing and what they are getting sounds good, makes them move, and most of all makes them feel good. After all, they're there to just have a good time, right? Wow. My brothers and sisters, please read for yourselves, study for yourselves, and think for yourselves.

Question: Could our pastors and church leaders actually be a hindrance to the spiritual growth of the church? Wow, what a thought. In a case like this, the answer comes roaring back with a resounding "Absolutely." He is a cleverly disguised deceiver; an impressive imposter; and a polished pretender. My dear brothers and sisters, I say to you, please open your eyes.

There are some who eventually decided that enough was enough and that they had taken all they could take of meaningless mottos, sermons without substance, and fruitless activity. These individuals finally realized that what they were involved in week after week, in the name of Christian ministry, was in reality a counterfeit ministry. I truly believe that members of the body of Christ can sense when they are not hearing truth from the pulpit, although they may continue to attend for whatever reason. Some will leave that place because of it, but sadly most will remain. What I don't understand is why.

Those who remain seem to be under some sort of spell that they can't escape or break free of. Their hearts and minds and their very souls, it seems, have been somewhat hypnotized and taken over by the pastor and his words, to the point that they no longer have the ability or even the desire to think for themselves. They are now under his spell, and they will believe and do whatever he tells them, without thinking, without question, and without hesitation. He absolutely has the members so much under his power that they couldn't break free of it even if they wanted to. Isn't this one attribute of a cult?

Almost everywhere I look, I see individuals who never grow in their understanding of the Word of God or in their desire to know more about the Word of God, yet they continue to come to church week after week. They seem to have no desire to know any more about what God wants them to know than what they've already learned. They seem to be content to remain at the same level spiritually as they were years ago. They genuinely believe they are getting everything they need (certainly everything they want) when they come and receive their weekly dose of emotional stimulation, entertainment, philosophy, and scriptural error. For them, this experience has produced a sense of fulfillment that they have done their Christian duty and are now prepared for the week ahead.

From time to time, I hear expressions of concern from some pastors and members that the church is not growing. And in their eyes, since the church is not growing, that means we need to step it up a notch. It means we need to do more of what we're doing. And if we still don't get results, then we need to incorporate some of the world's growth models, expansion methods, and development techniques in order to grow the church. Are we so spiritually dense to think that God needs the wisdom of fallen man in order to assist him in this incomprehensible divine undertaking? Wow. Our concern should be about growing up the individual believer, but instead we are more concerned about growing the size of worship centers and congregations.

So many of the members that we already have are afflicted with severely stunted growth, but instead of focusing on growing up the ninety-nine, we feverishly engage in activity that we think and hope will attract one more member in order to make the number be one hundred. Truly amazing. But of course growing up and maturing the saints might result in them becoming less dependent on the pastor and the religious system he has set up, and we wouldn't want that now, would we?

Here's an idea: Let's leave growing the size of God's church to God and let us stay out of it. Instead of trying to grow the church, why not spend all of our time and concentrate all of our energies on perfecting the saints for the work of the ministry, for the edifying of the body of Christ (Ephesians 4:12). We have been deceived into thinking that the larger the church, the more spiritual it is. We need to understand that the size of the congregation is no indication of God's endorsement, approval, or blessing, for that matter. Neither is it our responsibility to increase its size.

Growing the physical size of the church is God's concern. That is something that is completely up to him. He is the one who has determined how large it's going to be. He is the one who adds to the church those who are being saved, and thank God that he does because we often add to the church those who are not saved. We (and I emphasize "we") have made it easier to become part of the church than God has made it by stating that all you have to do is walk down the aisle, give the pastor your hand, answer one or two questions that pops into his head from who knows where (certainly not from the Word of God), and you're in. I don't think we will ever figure out that church growth is in God's hands, not ours.

But even when we speak of growing the size of the church, we speak of it so selfishly because our concern is not about the worldwide church; the universal church; the invisible church. But it is only about the local gathering which we attend. Our motives are truly impure, and our desires are selfish ones because we only want to grow our church just enough so that it is larger than the one across or down the street. Wow.

Our pastors and church leaders have developed a system that actually discourages members from using their minds. It appears that they do not want their members to read or study the Word for themselves as God has designed. Apostle Paul, in Romans 12:2, encourages us to "be ye transformed by the renewing of your mind" and to "be renewed in the spirit of your mind" (Ephesians 4:23). Are you kidding me? There might just as well be a sign posted as you enter the building: "Thinking Not Allowed." God help us. The shared thinking in our churches is that it's preferable to study books about the Bible because they make for easier understanding. The only thing I can say is that statement is completely untrue, absolutely unbelievable. Transformation and renewal of our mind can only come from reading and studying the Word of God. I dare you to try it.

After being indoctrinated all these decades by nonbiblical sermons, unscriptural music, and pure mindless emotion, nothing more than extreme external stimulation, outward activity and all-out sensationalism, there is a net benefit for the inner man of zero.

So if we use the scriptures as our standard when we consider these things, the black church today continues to be this truly spiritually irrelevant and ineffective entity that meets week after week with no intentions of ever becoming the church of scripture that it claims to be.

I pray that my people will soon open their eyes to the truth that God is trying to show them.

# 3

# THE WORK OF THE CHURCH OR CHURCH WORK?

In Romans 10:2, the apostle Paul gives Israel credit for having "a zeal of God." But he quickly points out that although their zeal was genuine, it was not according to knowledge. He states that they, being ignorant of God's righteousness and going about to establish their own righteousness, had not submitted themselves to the righteousness of God.

The black church finds itself in a similar position as Israel. We are a busy church, and there has always been an incredible amount of activity associated with it. But similar to the example of Israel, yes, we are zealous as well, but the activity we are so passionately involved in is not according to truth. We have proven by our actions that we are ignorant of God's truth and have worked to establish our own truth and have not submitted ourselves to the truth of God's Word. Although what can be observed in our churches is considered to be the work of the church, it is, in fact, not the work of the church at all. It is instead what I call "church work."

Practically all of the activities that take place in our churches, as sincere as they may appear (most of the time), accomplish absolutely no Godly edifying and no spiritual benefit to the individual believer or to the church, according to the scripture. For some, doing this work seems to give them a feeling of elevated spirituality and makes them feel good about themselves simply because they did it. Sadly, they do not realize that it does nothing to perfect them for the work of the ministry, for the edifying of the body of Christ. This church work consists of numerous services, activities, and programs that our pastors and leaders have created and are designed to grow us up spiritually and to make us more worthy of God's blessings than those who do not participate.

The black church is totally off base and completely off the biblical track when it comes to the mission and task the church has been given. It's not even close. The black church is way out in left field, or to be more exact, way over in another field, doing something else that the church was never set up or instructed to do. And the saddest thing about this is that the members do not recognize that they are involved in totally worthless and useless activity. So they continue to attend, week after week, for more of the same, totally oblivious to the things they should be doing as a legitimate scriptural church.

They are not aware of what the scripture says about these things because they are never told, and they are never encouraged to read and study for themselves. In a way, members are not encouraged to study the scripture; instead, they are encouraged to attend nonbiblical "Bible" classes where courses based on books about the Bible instead of the Bible itself. Oh, there is traditional Sunday school and a variety of Bible classes here and there, where students can get involved in a variety of discussions. Everybody is free to give their opinion about a particular passage of scripture or give accounts of related experiences they've had. So it's not at all a true study of the scripture, in any sense of the word. Thank God, there are some who have been able to recognize this and have moved on to other places. Those who remain see nothing wrong and believe that everything is fine.

What appears to have actually happened is that our pastors and church leaders have failed to provide the church with what it needs in order for its members to grow and mature and for the church to develop as a biblical church should. The true work of the church, according to Ephesians 4:12, is "the perfecting of the saints, for the work of the ministry, for the edifying of the body of Christ." How much plainer or simpler could it be? There seems to be a deliberate effort on the part of pastors and church leaders to take advantage of or to manipulate and deceive its members.

Church work in the black church is what our pastors and church leaders have determined is needed or is necessary for the church to be legitimate. All these things are done in order to maintain a religious tradition, uphold denominational beliefs, and promote a personal philosophy. This agenda is nothing more than a ton of activities that they have created and have absolutely nothing to do with the work of the church as laid out in scripture. It is merely church work. These activities do nothing more than waste people's time and completely tire them out. This is work that the local church has taken upon itself to do, for reasons outside of the scripture, simply because the pastor, church leaders, or some committee decided that it needed to be done. Read for yourself, study for yourself, and think for yourself.

Most of the programs that we are encouraged to participate in will never be found in the scripture. No matter how thoroughly you search, you won't find them. Go ahead … look. It appears that our pastors and leaders have become so smart that they've figured out that God, in laying out his agenda for the church, forgot something. They determined that he overlooked something. They discovered that God left something out. In their investigation of the scriptures, they found out that God totally missed something, and they decided that it was necessary to point out to him what he has missed. They are now in the process of showing him just exactly where he went wrong. This is why they have come up with the many additional programs that have been put in place in order for him to be successful in what he's been trying to accomplish all this time.

We as the church believe that we have designed a more effective agenda than the one God gave us in scripture. So we say, "Don't worry about it, God; we've got this." Therefore, we invent and create church programs, activities, auxiliaries, and services galore and encourage people to get involved so that we can grow the church. What? Are we kidding ourselves?

So church work in the black church is work that we see as necessary; it's just that God forgot to mention or didn't have the foresight to realize that it would be needed further down the road. For the most part, those who participate seem to experience some enjoyment in performing these activities, and even if it physically tires them out, it makes them feel spiritual, and they feel that others, especially the pastor, will see them as spiritual individuals, or they have been told they will gain God's favor by doing these things. They are also led to believe that unless they do these things, they won't get all of the blessings that God has for them.

Why in the world would a church that has one well-attended service, add a second service that it doesn't need, that never really takes off from an attendance standpoint, and is in fact very poorly attended, even after a number of years, apparently just so that it can say "we offer two services." And in addition to that, occasionally and in some instances quite frequently invite another church or attend another church at three o'clock in the afternoon for a third service? And I have actually seen an additional evening service that follows the first three services. Are you kidding me? Well, why not let's have a fifth and sixth service, as well? If four services in one day are good, then of course five or six would be even better. Right?

Make no mistake: You can never have too many church services. Right? Especially on Sunday; it's as if God is going to reward us according to the amount of time we spend not "at the cross" but "at the church." Our pastors and leaders have led us to believe that we will earn additional divine points or spiritual credits based upon the number of church services we attend. This kind of thinking is completely unscriptural, and it is absolute spiritual insanity. O God, please help us, Lord. How many services does a person really need? Somebody please tell me; God, help us. My dear reader, read for yourself, study for yourself, and think for yourself.

In order to make the extra services appear to be legitimate and so that they will sound impressive, you only need to give them a name. But the important thing is to just make sure you have the service. You can call it whatever you want: (1) anniversary, (2) pastor's anniversary, (3) pastor and wife's anniversary, (4) church anniversary, (5) Sunday school day, (6) women's day (7) men's day, (8) usher's day, (9) youth day, (10) black history day (what? Black history day? In the church? Oh well; hey, what about church history? Can't find it. Hmmm; something terribly wrong with that, but let's continue: (11) note burning, and (12) sacrificial day. Wow, how incredibly self-centered and self-absorbed can the church be as to create services that highlight, emphasize, point out, and celebrate not what God has done but what we have done, what our pastors have done, or what certain members have done. We just love to pat each other on the back and tell ourselves what wonderful Christians we are.

We are absolutely, totally, completely, and hopelessly addicted not to Christ, not to the Word, but to church programs and services. Let's be completely honest: We are not about exalting Christ. And we are not about exalting the Word of God. We are all about ourselves, and we have exalted ourselves above Christ and above the Word of God. We are our final authority. Wow. We would all do well to consider some familiar words of a well-known Bible character found in the book of Isaiah 14:13-14, who said, "I will exalt my throne above the stars of God," "I will ascend above the heights of the clouds," and "I will be like the most high." Absolutely amazing; my dear reader, please read for yourself, study for yourself, and think for yourself.

And let's not forget about the revivals, seminars, and conferences that we say we have in order to spiritually benefit the people, but the only thing they do is bring in some high-profile, popular speaker who does nothing more than entertain the people. If the pastor's ministry is truly in such poor condition that it needs to be supplemented by inviting someone to come in and speak, then that pastor has failed in carrying out his ministerial duties and needs to step down immediately.

And whatever you do, don't forget the myriad of auxiliaries that slipped God's memory. He simply forgot to tell us to set these things up. Thank God we figured out on our own that we needed them: (1) brotherhood, (2) women's ministry, (3) Bible institute (this could be another book), and (4) Sunday school (a very loose term). And of course, our music, which will definitely be another book. Musicals galore: (1) adult musical, (2) youth musical, (3) children's musical, (4) male chorus musical, (5) women's ministry musical, and (6) dance ministry. I've even heard of a midnight musical. If the church needs supplemental services or activities (give them any name you want), then it needs to seriously consider a complete makeover from the ground up, because its basic and primary function is a complete failure.

When you take a good look at the black church, you will see a tremendous amount of activity but very little ministry, if any at all. And even though you observe people who are very enthusiastic, what they do is totally unrelated to and has nothing at all to do with the work of the church, the body of Christ. Somehow, we seem to have this insatiable desire to be busy doing something, anything; we only need to make sure it looks and sounds religious, and the people will accept it.

Family time is a foreign concept in the church. And because it is it never is considered, and therefore no value is placed on it. How many families have been stressed, strained, and torn as a direct result of family members being obligated to be involved in extra church meetings that were totally unnecessary (and neither were they spiritually beneficial in any way). In cases like this, could the church possibly be an enemy of the family unit that it is supposed to promote and support?

It seems that we have never figured out what the true work of the church is. We simply do not have a clue, although the scriptures provide us with very clear instructions. We never understood that the true work of the church takes place outside the four walls of the church building, not on the inside. But in so many cases, we are so completely physically and mentally worn out from what we've been involved in on the inside that we can't be as effective as we need to be on the outside. Please open our eyes, Lord.

We also need to beware of our premature celebrating of apparent successes that have resulted from this work. It's not celebration time for the church, anyway. The church is nowhere near done with its work yet. God will let us know when. It is one thing to be able to say, "Look at all the wonderful things we've accomplished and in such a short time," but sadly, what about all the needless casualties and fatalities (physical and spiritual) that have resulted in the process? Also, can you say that those things that were accomplished were truly on the church's list of things to do? Or were they things on the pastor's and church leaders' list of things they wanted done? We are simply too concerned about nonchurch deeds to the point that we have abandoned the true work of the church and embraced self-centered accomplishments instead.

There is an unwillingness and an inability in our pastors and leaders to properly teach and instruct members of the body of Christ, and as a result, as new members have joined with us, they have brought their naturalistic, secular thinking along with them. And since they do not receive proper teaching, instruction, or training according to the scriptures, the results have been and will continue to be disastrous and devastating. In some cases, the effects of their influence may not be immediately realized, but it will show up in some form somewhere down the road.

So the church continues to be this lively but sadly irrelevant, ineffective entity with no intentions of trying to correct itself or improve because it doesn't realize that it needs to. The church, although not perfect, should be comprised of true believers (as much as we can tell) who are being perfected for the work of the ministry, for the edification of the body of Christ. If the church intends to be who it has been called to be, then it is urgent that it takes another look at the scriptures and realizes who it is and that it should do away with trying to be everything else *but* the church. God help us.

It would serve us all well to remember that no matter how strongly you feel about something, if it does nothing to perfect the saints for the work of the ministry, then don't be involved in it. If it doesn't exalt Christ or the Word of God, then have absolutely nothing to do with it.

In the world today, the adversary, who is the god of this world (2 Corinthians 4:4), is hard at work promoting "the lie" program of rejecting what God has said in his Word and promoting the opposite, that of being our own final authority. We should never underestimate just how clever, how deceptive, and how good the enemy really is at what he does. So don't be tricked, as so many have been, into assisting him. Jesus brought a very cutting but very appropriate charge against the religious leaders of Israel when he told them they had turned his house of prayer into a den of thieves (Matthew 21:12, 13). When we consider the activities of selling and buying in the temple that was taking place, that house of prayer existed in name only. What an absolutely accurate and fitting example of gross abuse.

When we consider what the church is truly called to be and represent, as opposed to what it actually is and does, what have our churches become dens of? We are merely impersonating the church (and not even doing a good job of that). More accurately, I should say we are the church in name only. We have a sign out in front of the building, but that's all we've got. The church has a definite mission, a definite calling, and a definite purpose. Why not let's engage in it? How about making it a priority? Let's not settle for simply setting up various church activities and being involved in them just to be busy. Get busy, yes, but get busy doing the work of the church, the body of Christ. Get busy doing what God is doing in this age of grace.

We live in a fallen world, and man is a fallen creature. And as a consequence, it is inevitable that we will have problems in this life. But we need to realize that God is fully aware of this, and he is working a plan that he set in motion a long time ago. All that we see around us and all that we experience is a part of that plan (a small part, I might add). And he doesn't need suggestions or ideas, certainly not from us. But just suppose God did need help with something. Do you really believe that he would be interested in anything we could conceive in our finite minds? I think not.

Why does the black church feel it needs to solve the racial problem? Why does it feel that it can? Where does that mentality originate from? God never intended for the church, certainly not the black church, to right all the wrongs in the world, not even the wrongs that have been done to the black race. He never intended for us to correct all of the ills of society. No matter how thoroughly we search, that is something we won't find in the scriptures. The church, black, white, or any other color, just needs to be the church ... please.

Forgive us, Lord; we've never figured out what we were supposed to do, although it is stated very clearly in your Word. We've totally missed it, and we keep missing it. We say with our mouths that it's all about you, Lord, but in our hearts, in our speech, and in our actions, we say with a loud voice, "It's all about us."

The church doesn't need to become any other organization except the church. It doesn't need to be the Red Cross or the United Way or the United Nations. We don't need to become the NAACP. We don't even need to be a political party. We simply need to be the church.

Why would the church want to be something other than what it is? I believe it is simply because it doesn't understand who and what it is. This completely misguided passion can be observed in many of our pastors and church leaders. I urge you, dear reader: Read for yourself, study for yourself, and think for yourself.

Just in case you didn't know, the church of scripture has been given a script to follow. We cannot afford to deviate from that script by coming up with something popular or culturally palatable or appealing. Our problem is that we keep trying to come up with something that will benefit our people only, something that we think will meet the approval of our people. What? What about God's approval? We only need to be the church. I am reminded of a song that is very true. The title simply says "Let the Church Be the Church."

My dear reader, if you are a Christian, then be a Christian. But you need to know what that means, according to the scripture and not according to what you have been told. We've all complained about something that we purchased, that turned out to be different from what it was advertised as. What about you? If you are truly not a Christian, you may deceive some people, but you can't deceive God, and you had better think twice about trying to deceive a discerning Christian.

If you are not a Christian, then maybe that's not a priority with you. But I would strongly advise you to believe the gospel according to 1 Corinthians 15:3, 4.

# 4

# THE PREACHING OF FOOLISHNESS

The subject of preaching in the black church is something that could fill an entire book all by itself. You can't talk about black preaching without talking about the entertaining style and the nonbiblical message that characterizes it. People flock to hear great speakers who can move the crowd with their words but say basically nothing according to the rightly divided truth of the Word of God. The preacher preaches what he feels, not what the scriptures proclaim. Although he will read a particular scripture as the text of the sermon, he will then begin to talk about something totally different from what he just read.

As you listen, you will hear opinion, philosophy, and cultural tradition spoken. Even though the minister claims to give you a word from the Lord, you will instantly realize that it is everything but a Word from the Lord. What you will typically hear is a word from his human mind, which can never fulfil the desires of your inner self. You will walk away from that service emotionally filled but spiritually empty. And because it does move the people and make them feel good, they cheer him on. The more he gives them, the more they want. It is as though this experience were some type of narcotic. The fact that the words he speaks go totally contrary to the scriptures doesn't seem to bother the people at all. Truly amazing.

In 1 Corinthians 1:21, Paul uses a term that is very interesting. He speaks of "the foolishness of preaching." While I make no attempts to compare what Paul is speaking of with what I am trying to say here, by putting a bit of a twist on the phrase "the foolishness of preaching," the perfect description of what goes on in the pulpit of the average black church is what I call "the preaching of foolishness." If you expect to hear the Word of God spoken from the pulpit of many of today's black churches, chances are you're gonna be sadly disappointed. Black preaching in our churches seems to consist of nothing more than passing on of cultural traditions; being politically and racially correct; making clever sayings; cracking jokes; entertaining; performing; emotionalizing; promoting the black race; staying on top of civil rights issues; promoting social justice; advancing black ideology, black philosophy, and black theology; sharing personal feelings; and everything but the true Word of God. Wow. In the church?

When you take a close look at the black church in general, you will see an unbiblical religious system that is set up in order to provide pastors with a place to indoctrinate, promote, and spread cultural tradition and philosophy that has been passed down for generations. This is all done in the name of Christianity. The preacher's only objective is to quench the members' thirst to be entertained and emotionally stimulated, and to fulfill their desire to be externally excited. And because this has continued down through the years, the black church as a result never became the legitimate spiritual entity that the church is called to be.

Most of our people have never been given the opportunity to experience the true reality of the faith they claim to possess. Because basically nothing they hear from the pulpit on Sunday morning can be validated or verified by the rightly divided Word of God. Therefore, my heart's desire and prayer to God for my people is that they read for themselves, study for themselves, and think for themselves. Then and only then can we realize and come to understand the wonderful message God has given specifically to us (the church, the body of Christ) in this age of grace. This is our only hope because I fear that we will never expect to get the truth from our church leaders.

Traditionally, the preacher's role on Sunday morning has been to begin where the music stops; he needs to be prepared to take the service up from there by speaking in a style that entertains the waiting congregation. Whether or not the words are based on the Word of God is of no importance, as far as the worshippers are concerned. He can say pretty much anything he wants and get away with it. He needs only to say it in an entertaining way.

As I was growing up, I never heard a pastor or teacher say anything about God's overall plan of exalting his Son in heaven and on the earth and how we as the church would fit into that plan. I don't think any of them ever knew.

I know that the black church is unquestionably capable of understanding spiritual things, but the problem is that they have never been exposed to the key truths of God's Word, which give us spiritual perspective. Saints can never be perfected and edified if they are never presented the Word of God to allow it to work as it is designed to.

It seems that black pastors and teachers (either deliberately or unknowingly) keep their members uninformed and in the dark about the true ways of God, and as a result, many black Christians (if they are indeed Christians) have no idea who they are in Christ or what they're supposed to be doing. They don't even know that they are in Christ or what that exactly means. They are ill-equipped saints and are spiritually unfit to do the work of the church. I believe the pastors and church leaders are engaged in an ongoing effort to prevent the members from finding out the truth of scripture. Could it be that the people in our churches are being isolated from the truth so that they remain dependent upon the pastors and leaders? If so, then pastors and church leaders will continue to control the thinking of its people and thereby control its people.

The black preacher through his preaching has steered us forever in the wrong spiritual direction. He has led us down the path of anti-truth. He has not given us as believers what our inner man has truly yearned for. Instead of edifying us, he has only entertained us, and as a result, our spiritual growth has suffered immensely and is severely stunted at best. In 2 Corinthians 4:16, the apostle Paul says, "For which cause we faint not; but though our outward man perish, yet the inward *man* is renewed day by day." And again in Ephesians 3:16, "That he would grant you, according to the riches of his glory, to be strengthened with might by his Spirit in the inner man."

Preaching in the black church by its very nature absolutely plays on our emotional make-up, never taking into account the presence, desires, and needs of the inner person (or the inward man, as Paul describes him). But thanks be to God, we can recover. Read for yourself, study for yourself, and think for yourself.

We as a people love to entertain and be entertained. And we see our church service as just another legitimate form of entertainment, in many ways, like any other form of entertainment; if we call it "church," then we feel that it is our step up or our step toward God for the week. So we take care of what's required of us spiritually on Sunday and then go back to our Monday-through-Saturday routine, and that's the way the week usually goes. Most people enjoy things that amuse and things that entertain. Our people seem to have this craving for hype, emotional stimulation, sensationalism, over the top, off the wall, and the desire for the wild and crazed experience. Make no mistake: It is our make-up. It is who we are. And whatever we do, there you will find these components included in it, yes even in church.

But the true purpose of preaching is not to entertain, yet that is precisely what you will get in most black churches. And that is exactly what the people want. If the preacher can't whoop, then according to the black church, the official but usually unspoken verdict is that he doesn't possess preaching skills. It is usually said, "He can't preach." Wow. And although it is unspoken, it will surely be very clearly communicated to him in some way.

After the sermon has been preached, if nobody walks the aisle during the invitational time, then the invitation song must not have been long enough. Therefore, we need to sing one more verse (or maybe even an additional song), and then they will come.

On one Sunday, an unsaved relative of a member was visiting the church, as he had done several times before. During the invitational part of the service, during the singing of the song, the preacher came down out of the pulpit area, walked down the aisle, and stood less than two feet from the individual; face to face, with arms outstretched toward the man, he literally begged him to come and join the church. I thought, *Wow.*

So maybe we should sing as many verses of the invitational song as is necessary until somebody comes. We believe that we haven't had church unless somebody walks down that aisle. Having the preacher give us biblical truth during the sermon was not the issue. If nobody came down that aisle, then the preacher didn't preach or the choir didn't sing.

I pray that God will give my people a desire to read and study his Word for themselves and that they might see the wonderful truths that he has for us but have been hidden from us.

# 5

## TEACHING

Paul says to us in 2 Timothy 2:2 "and the things that thou hast heard of me ... the same commit thou to faithful men, who shall be able to teach others also." Legitimate teaching in the church according to the scripture is the taking of the things given to us by God through Paul (who is our apostle, by the way, according to Romans 11:13) and committing those things to faithful men, who shall be able to teach others also. The qualified teacher, according to Paul, is one who is faithful in that he has learned the truth of scripture and is able to teach others also. So the teacher must have received the truth, not tradition, not life experience, not that which is interesting, and not simply what has been handed down, but scriptural truth, and he is able to teach others also. To receive the truth is good, but it's not enough. He must be able to faithfully communicate that same truth without deviation to others.

Therefore, those who teach the Word of God must of necessity be knowledgeable of the Word of God, given to us through Paul. And to be knowledgeable of the Word of God is to understand it rightly divided (2 Timothy 2:15). Then and only then can proper teaching and learning according to the scripture take place. In the church, the body of Christ, proper teaching of the Word is primary and must take top priority above everything else. Nothing should be allowed to take its place. Everything else stems from it.

But as far as I have been able to observe, true biblical teaching is practically nonexistent in the black church. I know there is the traditional Sunday school and maybe a Bible class or two; the traditional Wednesday night Bible study is quite common, and in some instances, a Bible institute here and there. But even those classes exist in name only for the most part, when you consider the fact that very few (if any) biblical truths are communicated during class time. I have attended classes that were advertised as Bible classes that were not Bible classes at all but were in fact something you'd expect to find offered at the local community college; they had nothing to do with the Bible. And even the few somewhat legitimate Bible courses that do exist are typically taught by individuals who are totally untrained and unknowledgeable of the course they are teaching. They were just simply asked to teach a course because there was a need for teachers, and they were available.

I would describe these Bible classes as nothing more than a coming together of individuals to express their differing thoughts on the scripture. In the classes that I have attended, you will only hear the instructor's ideas and the students' concepts about what they think the scripture is saying in their opinion. There is no genuine study of the scriptures itself. A true examination of the scripture in order to see what it actually teaches never takes place. Teaching it seems has always taken a back seat to preaching in the black church. Preaching because it is more exciting, entertaining, and emotionally stimulating is understandably more popular, more accepted, and more encouraged than teaching. It also has much higher attendance. I haven't decided if that's a good thing or a bad thing.

Whether it is Sunday school or another Bible class, individuals are asked to teach even though they do not have the qualifications to teach. The philosophy, it seems, is when you need somebody to do something in the church, be it teach or whatever, just grab the first person who walks by. Just get anybody to do it so you can say that the church does offer that particular ministry or class or whatever. Just get anybody who will agree to do it. Don't waste valuable time trying to figure out if they are qualified or if they are trained or whether they even want to do the job. If they are within an arm's reach distance, then they're qualified. If they breathe oxygen, then they're qualified, so sign them up.

I've talked with some people who really had no desire to teach or head up an auxiliary because they didn't feel they were qualified. They just didn't feel comfortable doing it because they had not been trained. But they were encouraged to do it anyway because they were needed. Is there any wonder why the black church is in the state it's in? In our churches today, there can be found little evidence of an intelligent understanding of the Word of God among its members, including the clergy. This is tremendously disturbing to me. If there is not a proper understanding of the word of God among the ranks of our leaders, then how can the truth be taught to the people? Well, the answer is, it can't be. So I strongly and prayerfully urge you, dear reader: Read for yourself, study for yourself, and think for yourself. Because clearly, to spiritually edify the believer is not the primary objective of the black church. And in its current state, it is utterly incapable of doing it. And worse: It has neither the interest in changing nor the desire to do so.

There is a famous movie line that says, "You can't handle the truth." But in the case of the black church, it's not "We can't handle the truth," because we certainly can. But we have overwhelmingly demonstrated that "we don't want the truth." And since we don't want the truth, no one had better dare try and give us the truth. John 8:32 says, "And the truth shall make you free," but we as a people have demonstrated, at least from a religious standpoint, that we do not want to be made free. We as a people are comfortable where we are; we don't want to change, nor do we feel the need to change. We are satisfied with where we are on our spiritual journey. We are content in our thinking, our beliefs, our culture, and our traditions. Don't offer us any meat. We are completely satisfied with our milk. Freedom would force us to abandon all those things and many more that make us who we are.

We in the black church were never taught who the biblical Holy Spirit truly is. We were taught that the Holy Spirit was an "It." We never knew he was a person. We never knew he was a member of the Godhead, equal to the Father and the Son, with the same attributes. We have been taught that if you become emotional enough, "It" will make you cry, shout, run, jump, or yell. We have always been taught that you could feel the Holy Spirit. We were taught that when the Holy Spirit hits you, then you will shout or move or make some type of emotional expression.

Being a Christian is not a feeling, whether you're at church or any place else. But it is a fact based on the truth of the Word of God. However, we've been taught for decades and decades that the Holy Spirit is something you can feel in your emotions, and if you have it, then you can feel it. We have also been taught that the more emotional you are in the church service, then the more of the Holy Spirit you have and consequentially the more spiritual you are. Really?

Maybe you do experience a feeling during the church service, and maybe you do become emotional, but that feeling and that emotion is not the Holy Spirit. The way we know that the Holy Spirit is present in the life of the believer is by observing the very specific fruit that he produces in our lives. Apostle Paul lists them in Galatians 5:22. I want to say to you, dear reader: Don't trust your feelings. If any of you are *Star Wars* fans, I say to you Obiwan lied to you. Your feelings can and will deceive you, so don't trust them.

I feel so sorry for people who have been deceived and misled to believe that the only thing the Holy Spirit was sent to do was to make you move and give you a good feeling in your emotions while you are at church. I'm not knocking emotions and feelings. What I am saying is that what you experience and feel in your emotions is real, but it is not the Holy Spirit, and it is not God. Instead you have allowed your emotions to become your god. Therefore, whenever you come to church and do not get that feeling, then you feel you haven't worshipped.

We were never taught that we could and should think for ourselves, but we were always told what to think about the scripture. And if it was discovered that someone came up with an independent thought, then they were immediately encouraged to discard that thought and to accept the official correct thought: the traditional, handed-down, cultural one. Wow.

Over the years, I have had the opportunity to see many things in the black church. I've even seen racial hatred and prejudice promoted in the church, which is bad enough, but I would never have believed that I would hear racial hatred preached from the pulpit. I have. From the pulpit. I was in total shock. I could not believe my ears. I was stunned. I was petrified. It was as though everything stood perfectly still for a moment. It was as if I had entered a void zone of some type. There seemed to be absolute, complete silence all around. At that point, I realized just how dense the spiritual darkness can be in so many of our black churches, right in the midst of very lively spiritual activity.

We have no problem with promoting racism right from the pulpit because we have failed to see that according to the scriptures, there is only one race in the church the body of Christ. We have failed to see that according to Galatians 3:28, "there is neither Jew nor Greek ... for ye are all one in Christ Jesus." We have never figured out, even as the church, that the fallen human heart is the reason for racial prejudice, inequality, social injustice, or any other problems that appear to be highlighted or accented by race. Instead, we have decided that even though God couldn't figure it out, we realized that we had a racial problem, and we were going to single-handedly tackle it. The black church needs to understand that yes, the black race does have an enemy; but is not the white race. We have a very real enemy who has been around a lot longer than the white race. In fact, he's been around a lot longer than man, period. We have a genuine enemy; we have a common enemy: the adversary. Fight him. Don't assist him. This is something that the true church of all races and creeds needs to realize.

We are totally consumed with attempting to right all of society's wrongs, mainly those that have to do with social injustice and racial inequality, so much so that fixing the world's problems has become our primary reason for existence, when it should be perfecting the saints for the work of the ministry, for the edifying of the body of Christ. Are we the church or aren't we? What are we thinking? Our preoccupation with race has totally blinded us to the truth of scripture. Yes, these problems do exist, but I would like to remind you, my brothers and my sisters, God is totally aware of all these things.

What I am saying to our pastors and church leaders is that if you are so passionate about all of these things, then you need to launch a movement (and some have) that will be set up in order to fight against these things or get involved in one that already exists, but whatever you do, don't refer to yourself as the church. Remove that "church" sign from the front of your building because that's not who or what you are. The church has quite a different agenda. God has set it, and you desperately need to become acquainted with it and adhere to it … that is, if you intend to be the church of scripture.

# 6

# THE BLACK CHURCH RELIGION

The black church today is about nothing more than coming together just to have a good time; nothing more. My dear reader, beware of a feel-good gospel or a feel-good religion or a feel-good experience. I have come to see in my time that the gathering of the saints on Sunday in the black church, for the most part, is mainly just an event. It is something that we have designed, we have created, and we have developed for the people to come and be amused. To borrow a phrase, it is absolutely "of the people, by the people, and for the people." That's nothing to be proud of, by the way, because if that is true, and it is, then it is not of God.

From the preaching to the music to the singing to the programs and all the many insignificant activities, the best thing that I can say about the black church is that over all these years, I have learned a lot of jokes. So it's not been a total waste. On a typical Sunday morning, if you're sitting in the congregation at many of our churches, you will most likely be thoroughly entertained, but there is a high probability that you will not be spiritually edified, and your inner self will almost certainly leave that place in the same condition it was in when you arrived.

There is only one way to define the thinking, the mentality, and the activities that can be observed in the black church. It is not Christianity, but it is a religion. It is the black church religion. If we use the scriptures as the standard, then it is definitely not biblical Christianity. It is pure religion. It is religion because it requires one to do certain things and act in a certain way and say certain things in a certain way in order to receive God's blessings and favor. Down through the years, we have been indoctrinated and taught that we gain God's favor and receive spiritual merits by doing all of these things. We have been incorrectly taught that the more we perform, then the more spiritual we are. Since the black church religion is not of the scripture, it has no more merit than any other nonbiblical religion. And by the way, God has designed only one religion: Judaism.

We have made two very serious mistakes: (1) We took our traditions, culture, and experience, and created this thing we call Christianity. (2) We took a look at the scriptures and used the Christianity that we developed to define, interpret, and explain the scripture. As a result, we can only view the scripture through the lenses of our tradition. We have very carefully selected specific portions of the scripture that seem to fit our experience and support our beliefs and thinking, and we have used these scriptures in order to create our own religion. This is how we define our Christianity.

God revealed himself to the nation of Israel, but they rejected the only true God and chose to worship idols instead. God has given to the church very detailed information that is specific to us and about us, concerning what he is doing today through us. But we have rejected that portion of the scripture because those scriptures oppose our thinking, tradition, and experience. They do not excite us, and neither do they emotionally stimulate us. So our rejection of God's specific instructions to us means that we have now become our own final authority. We have effectively changed the truth of God into a lie.

Our pastors and church leaders have deceived us, and we have deceived ourselves by elevating our emotions, feelings, intellect, and desire to be entertained above the truth. We are truly a religious people; we always were. We had to be. It seemed to help our ancestors endure the horrible things that they had to experience. We were a poor people, but we had religion. It was basically the only thing we had, so most of us were raised on religion. Many of us have raised our kids on it. But even though we were convinced in our hearts at that time it was truth, and even though we placed the highest value on it, it was not biblical. But we didn't know that it was not biblical. Our religious leaders (pastors or whatever) never knew, so how could the rest of us know? What we did in the name of religion were things we felt would someday elevate us out of the condition that we found ourselves in. We did things we thought were good, right, and Godly, which is basically true of all religions.

But now, even though illumination of God's Word continues and is more readily available than ever before to our pastors and church leaders, that former mind-set and thinking of the past continues until today. God's Word "to" the church has not found its way "into" the church. And consequently neither has it found its way into the heart of the individual church member. If our leaders have it, then they have not passed it on to us. But thank God, we as individuals need only to read for ourselves, study for ourselves, and think for ourselves. This is the way God intended it, according to Ephesians 3:4.

Since we don't take a serious look at the scriptures, we in the black church, whether pastor, church leader, or member, just don't know what we're supposed to do. We never knew. So we just say anything and do anything. We just say what we feel. We say what's on our hearts or we say what we think. We just speak whatever pops into our heads. We might look for a scripture that we think seems to support our thoughts; But only if we don't have to spend too much time searching for it. We just make it up as we go. Absolutely amazing.

I've even had the opportunity to hear a "counter-prayer" once. Can you believe it? A prayer was offered by one minister, and after he was done, the pastor immediately got up and gave a contradicting prayer; a prayer that was in direct opposition to the previous prayer. Wow. I thought, *What am I hearing? What?* I could not believe my ears. All of the foolishness is not found in the secular world. You will find much of it in the black church.

If we intend to operate under the banner of the church, then we must immediately get on the right track. We absolutely must give up this spiritual insanity that we are engaged in and become scriptural or find another title to operate under because we are certainly not the church.

Our unique church tradition is very powerful, and

although it is unscriptural, over time, it actually became our truth. Therefore, we embrace and hold on to it very tightly. And nothing stands a chance of separating us from it. But while this age of grace continues, the black church can still get on the right path. If only our people can be exposed to the true Word of God, then it can have the effect on us that God intended.

For the most part, our pastors and church leaders have so much invested in this colossal false indoctrination effort that they cannot afford to give it up now, even if they wanted to. This incredible deception has gone on far too long, and it's not likely that a change would come from that direction. So I plead with you, my brothers and my sisters, in the name of God. This is a matter of your soul. It is a matter of God the Father granting you, according to the riches of his glory, to be strengthened with might by his Spirit in the inner man (Ephesians 3:16).

Don't allow someone else to tell you what to think about the Word of God. Yes, we need pastors. Yes, we need teachers, but I ask you: Who's your final authority? I encourage you to be like the Berean believers of Acts 17:11, who were more noble than those in Thessalonica, in that they received the word with all readiness of mind and searched the scriptures daily, whether those things were so. Also in Ephesians 4:14, Paul admonishes us that we henceforth be no more children, tossed to and fro, and carried about with every wind of doctrine, by the sleight of men, and cunning craftiness, whereby they lie in wait to deceive. My dear reader, my prayer for you is that you recognize that God has spoken directly to you in his Word. I urge you to read for yourself, study for yourself, and think for yourself.

If the black church can come to see and understand from the scripture what the true mission of the church is, and if it can properly instruct its members accordingly, then it will be able to perfect the saints, for the work of the ministry, for the edifying of the body of Christ. If we can do this, then and only then will we be doing the true work of the church.

# SUMMARY

I see so many of my people in the church today who deep inside seem to be seeking, searching, and genuinely desiring the truth of the Word of God, but they have not received it. It is so unfortunate that there continues to be such an incredible waste of time and a gross misuse of a huge opportunity to spiritually edify the members of the church body of Christ.

Although God will accomplish his purpose in the church despite the church, I have come to see that the black church has failed in that (1) It has not recognized the true purpose of the church. (2) It has not produced perfected saints. (3) It has not exalted Christ or the Word of God. (4) It has exalted itself, its pastors, and certain individuals instead. (5) It has not spiritually educated the believers. (6) It has steered believers away from the scripture. (7) It has encouraged the believer not to study the scripture. (8) It has set up religious entertainment centers instead of churches. (9) It has adopted and promoted clichés rather than the Word of God. (10) It has made emotionalism synonymous with spirituality. (11) It has blinded its members to the true ways of the Spirit. (12) It has made social and political issues a priority while Godly edification remains a nonissue. (13)

And lastly and but most importantly, (14) It has not "rightly divided the Word of God," according to 2 Timothy 2:15.

Most importantly because, when the Word of God is rightly divided, we have God's approval, we are true workers, and we have no need to be ashamed. Dear reader, I urge you: Read for yourself, study for yourself, and think for yourself.

Printed in the United States
By Bookmasters